Remote Controls Are Better Than Women Because...

Or, What Men Would Say If They Dared

Karen Rostoker-Gruber

Illustrations by Don Smith

LONGSTREET PRESS
Atlanta, Georgia

Published by LONGSTREET PRESS, INC.,
a subsidiary of Cox Newspapers,
a division of Cox Enterprises, Inc.
2140 Newmarket Parkway
Suite 118
Marietta, Georgia 30067

Printed in the United States of America

1st printing, 1993

Library of Congress Catalog Number 92-84004

ISBN: 1-56352-076-1

This book was printed by Data Reproductions Corporation, Rochester Hills, Michigan.

Cover illustration and design by Rhino Graphics

This book is dedicated to my husband and my father,
who both drive me crazy when they use the remote control

Remote controls are better than women because . . .

they have a
mute button.

Remote controls are better than women because ...

you can swap them with your friends.

———

they never fake it.

———

you can always turn them on.

———

they don't get PMS.

Remote controls are better than women because...

you can always charge them up with a new
set of batteries.

===

you know exactly what you're in for when you
take them home with you.

===

you can pick them up morning, noon, or night.

Remote controls are better than women because . . .

they won't
saddle you
with in-laws.

Remote controls are better than women because ...

they don't care if the house is messy.

Remote controls are better than women because ...

you can replace them if they aren't working
up to your standards.

———

they don't complain about being used,
abused, or refused.

———

they can't reject you.

Remote controls are better than women because...

you don't have to pretend to be interested in
what they're saying.

Remote controls are better than women because...

you can touch them wherever you want and immediately get the desired result.

———

you can get one that glows in the dark.

———

they can't get pregnant.

Remote controls are better than women because...

you never have to tell them where you're going, when you're coming home, or who you're going out with.

Remote controls are better than women because . . .

they come with warranties and instruction manuals.

———

you can fool around with them in any
number of positions.

———

you can use them all night long.

Remote controls are better than women because...

they are as bright and cheery in the morning
as they are at night.

=====

when something goes wrong with them, there's
always a logical solution.

=====

they don't pressure you into getting married.

if you're attracted
to the one your
friend has,
you can get one
just like it.

Remote controls are better than women because...

they never care
what you look
like or what
you wear.

Remote controls are better than women because ...

it's okay if your friends pick them up
and play with them.

———

you can push their buttons as hard and
fast as you want to.

———

they are always home, right where you left them.

Remote controls are better than women because...

you have total
and complete
control over
them.

Remote controls are better than women because . . .

they give you a lifetime of pleasure, and you only
have to pay for them once.

———

they never talk about you with their friends.

———

they'll never leave the bedroom . . . if there's
a TV there.

you can have several in your house at one time,
and they won't get jealous.

=====

they don't get mad when you play with
them while watching TV.

=====

if you get rid of them, they don't come back.

Remote controls are better than women because . . .

they don't talk to you while you're watching football on TV.

17

they won't
leave the room
no matter what
rude or crude
things you are
doing.

Remote controls are better than women because...

they are always wired.

all of their sensitive spots are labeled for
your convenience.

they don't give ultimatums.

you don't have to buy them expensive dinners to get them to go home with you.

Remote controls are better than women because...

they never tell you what to do or how to do it.

===

they share your favorite pastime.

===

you can trade them in.

===

they don't eat, and they stay slim forever.

Remote controls are better than women because...

you can touch them whenever you want to, even
in front of your friends.

———

they don't snore.

———

technology continues to improve them.

Remote controls are better than women because . . .

you can play with two of them at the same time.

Remote controls are better than women because ...

they are always in the mood.

Remote controls are better than women because...

their buttons work even when they're cold.

———

they don't care how much money you make.

———

it doesn't bother them that you never stay on the
same channel for more than a second.

25

Remote controls are better than women because...

they don't make
you change the
channel when
a woman in a bikini
comes on TV.

26

Remote controls are better than women because...

you can shut them off.

———

they'll go home with you right away,
no questions asked.

———

they don't mind when you cheat on them
with another remote.

they look just as good the morning after.

Remote controls are better than women because...

you don't have to warn them that your
friends are coming over.

———

you never get nervous when you're with them.

———

you don't have to gaze into their eyes
when you touch them.

Remote controls are better than women because...

you can choose your favorite size, shape, and color.

===

they don't tease you.

===

you can order them through a catalog.

===

they don't tie up the telephone all day.

Remote controls are better than women because...

you never have to wait for them to get ready at night.

Remote controls are better than women because...

you don't have to remember their birthday.

32

Remote controls are better than women because...

they don't mind if you neglect them, although
you never will.

=====

they will lay perfectly still or assume whatever
position you put them in.

=====

they are absolutely dependent upon you.

33

Remote controls are better than women because . . .

you don't
have to buy
them flowers
the next day.

Remote controls are better than women because...

they can't get credit cards.

———

they won't use the sports section of the newspaper
to housebreak the dog.

———

you can play with them with one hand and
drink a beer with the other.

they are already flat on their back.

====

when you're lost and won't admit it, they won't insist that you stop and ask directions.

====

you can put them down or feel them up.

Remote controls are better than women because . . .

you don't have
to buy them
jewelry or furs.

Remote controls are better than women because...

they don't get upset when you drink directly out of the milk carton.

Remote controls are better than women because...

you can even sample them in the store.

═══

they don't complain when you leave the toilet seat up.

═══

they won't drive your new sports car
and grind the gears.

Remote controls are better than women because...

they don't require designer batteries.

=====

they never say, "Maybe we should just be friends."

=====

they don't call you at work and ask you to stop
by the store on the way home.

Remote controls are better than women because . . .

they don't make you say, "I love you, too," into the phone while you're at a card game with the boys.

Remote controls are better than women because...

they don't complain about your razor stubble
irritating their face.

Remote controls are better than women because...

you don't have to worry about them when they are at home alone with the plumber.

════

they don't spend money to get their nails wrapped.

════

they don't wake you up early Sunday morning to go food shopping.

Remote controls are better than women because ...

they don't play mind games with you.

Remote controls are better than women because . . .

they won't stand you up at the altar.

———

they don't volunteer your services to
their mothers.

———

once you've used one, you know how
to use them all.

they don't
make you
take dance
lessons.

Remote controls are better than women because...

they don't insist that you use protection.

———

you can open them up to see what
they're made of.

———

they don't scream at you when you
come home late.

Remote controls are better than women because...

you can put them away when you
don't want them.

———

they won't send you on guilt trips.

———

they don't buy clothes that go out of
style in two weeks.

they never recommend that you go on a diet.

Remote controls are better than women because . . .

they don't hang their pantyhose on the shower rod.

Remote controls are better than women because . . .

for a little more money, you can upgrade.

———

you can give them as presents.

———

they don't rehash their favorite soap opera.

———

they don't look through your dresser drawers.

they've never heard of Laura Ashley.

Remote controls are better than women because...

they don't embarrass you by calling you "honey"
in front of your friends.

───

they won't remind you that you haven't mowed
the lawn in four weeks.

───

they don't throw dishes at you.

Remote controls are better than women because...

they don't care if you throw your *new* red sweat
pants into the washing machine with all
the white underwear.

———

they don't mind seeing dirty dishes piled up in the sink.

———

if they fall apart, you just snap them back together.

they don't mind a few pretzel crumbs in bed.

Remote controls are better than women because ...

they never criticize your driving.

they don't wear fuzzy slippers.

=====

you can turn them on easily no matter what
size your fingers are.

=====

they don't have hairy legs.

they don't make you feel self-conscious when you take off your clothes.

Remote controls are better than women because...

they never comment on your
lame pick-up lines.

——

they don't drag you around to antique shops.

——

they don't collect ducks or owls.

Remote controls are better than women because...

they're just as happy on Naugahyde as chintz.

———

they don't care if you spill a little
beer on them.

———

they never borrow your razor.

Remote controls are better than women because . . .

you can use them for just a second and not worry
about how they judge your performance.

Remote controls are better than women because...

they don't have hair that "won't do a thing."

════

they don't walk through the house pointing out
all the stuff you've left lying around.

════

they don't cry on their birthdays.

Remote controls are better than women because...

they don't take up all the closet space.

Remote controls are better than women because . . .

you already
know they
can't cook.

Remote controls are better than women because ...

they don't kick you when you fall asleep and
roll over on top of them.

———

you don't have to call them everyday just
to say you love them.

———

they stay up as late as you do.

Remote controls are better than women because...

you can buy them at wholesale prices.

=====

they don't make you play with them any
longer than you want to.

=====

you can even get an imported model if
you want one.

Remote controls are better than women because . . .

they're never
too heavy to
hold in your lap.

Remote controls are better than women because...

they don't pack everything they own for
a weekend vacation.

Remote controls are better than women because...

they don't care whether or not you've showered
before you use them.

═══

they don't mind if you "touch and tell."

═══

they don't accuse you of forgetting to
water the houseplants.

Remote controls are better than women because...

there is always one waiting for you in a hotel room.

Remote controls are better than women because...

they never resent you for failing to do
more with your life.

⸻

they don't make sarcastic comments about
your friends.

⸻

they will never jilt you for another guy.

department store
sales are of no
more interest to
them than they
are to you.

Remote controls are better than women because...

they come with options.

───

you can always get the last word in.

───

they don't fantasize about other men
when you're with them.

Remote controls are better than women because...

they don't drag you home from parties just when you're starting to have a good time.

Remote controls are better than women because...

they never take the money out of your wallet.

═══

they don't need a different pair of shoes for
every day of the year.

Karen Rostoker-Gruber is also the author of
The Unofficial College Survival Guide.
She and her husband live in Bridgewater, New Jersey.